GRADE 1 VOCABULARY

Fun-filled Activities

An imprint of Om Books International

Words that Name Body Parts

Read the clues and fill in the crossword.

Across

1. You wear a cap on this
4. Used to eat and talk
6. This part helps you to sense sounds
7. The part of the body that gives you sight
8. Used to smell and breathe

Down

1. It is over your head and under your hat
2. Give shape to your body
3. We walk on these
5. You have it and the clock has it too–they are two in number

BONUS BOX

I have fingers and thumb but can't write. But I can keep you away from cold that's right. What am I?

Words that Name Accessories

Choose the correct word and circle it.

1. Kitty wears a bow on her **(forehead, hand, hair).**
2. Mr. Willie wears a belt around his **(elbow, thigh, waist).**
3. Mrs. Polly wears a ring on her **(toe, finger, nose).**
4. Lia wears a chain around her **(neck, body, arm).**
5. Peter wears a watch on his **(hand, wrist, knee).**

6. Ronny slings a bag over his **(shoulder, back, hip).**
7. Jane holds a seashell in her **(finger, teeth, palm).**
8. Mac took off his shoes and dip his **(feet, knees, ankles)** into the pond.

BONUS BOX

Use the words **heads, shoulders, knees** and **toes** to make a poem of your own. Sing it to the class.

What am I?

Tick the correct picture. Colour the letters to name the word which fits the description below.

I help the elephant splash, hold and lift things.

B	O	X	T	R	U	N	K	I	M

An octopus uses me to feel and grasp.

T	E	N	T	A	C	L	E	S	O

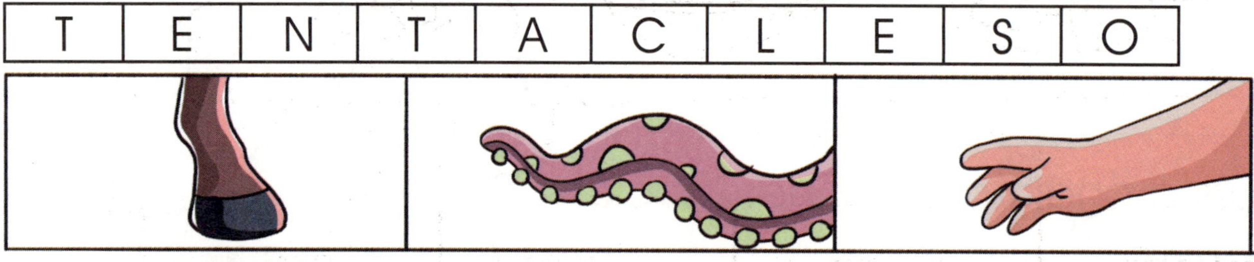

I allow fish to travel underwater.

L	E	G	S	F	I	N	S	I	G

A bird doesn't have teeth but I help it pick seeds

B	E	A	K	C	L	A	W	S	X

A tortoise hides inside me when senses danger.

H	O	O	D	S	H	E	L	L	O

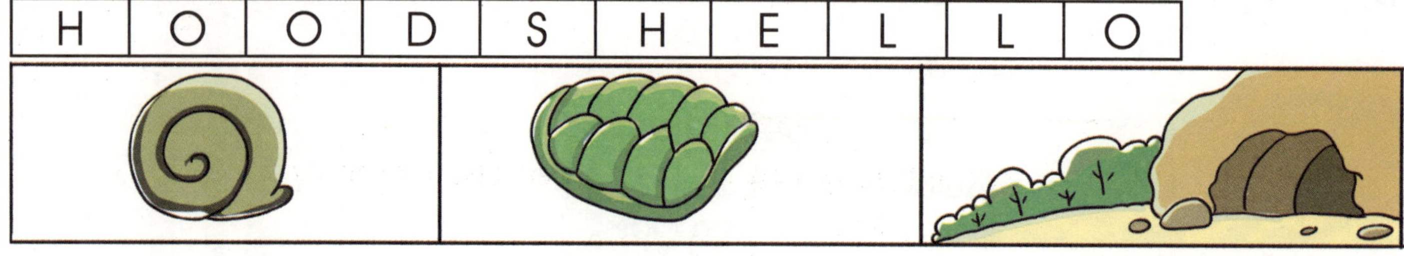

Words that Name People

Complete the family table by circling the boxes with words that name people.

father	plate	pet	cat
cap	boy	park	home
spoon	fruits	girl	mother

BONUS BOX

Make your family tree and write the names of your family members. Also paste their photographs.

Words that Name Clothes

Find these clothes words in the word search.
Look across, down and diagonally.

Socks	Skirt	Coat	Pants	Jacket	Shirt	Tie	Hat

a	b	c	d	e	f	g	j	h	s
i	s	o	c	k	s	j	a	k	h
l	k	m	o	n	o	p	c	q	i
r	i	p	a	n	t	s	k	s	r
t	r	u	t	v	w	x	e	y	t
z	t	a	b	c	d	e	t	f	g
h	i	j	k	l	m	n	o	p	q
t	i	e	r	s	t	h	a	t	u

BONUS BOX

I start with an A and end with an N. I'm something you wear when you are cooking. I keep your clothes spotless. What am I?

Off to Work

Read the words in the word bank. Write them to match the riddle.

teacher	dentist	policeman	fire fighter	architect	doctor

My job is to help you
when you are sick.
Being fit is my trick!

____

Classroom is my
place to be. You
learn a lot from me

____

I say, "Open wide"
And look at your
teeth inside.

____

Making plans is
what I do.
Building houses is
my job for you.

____

I help people when
stuck.
My tools are water,
hose and truck.

____

I am strong and
brave.
My job for all is to
save.

____

Words that Name Places

Help the bus reach the bus stop. Draw a line connecting all the words that name places.

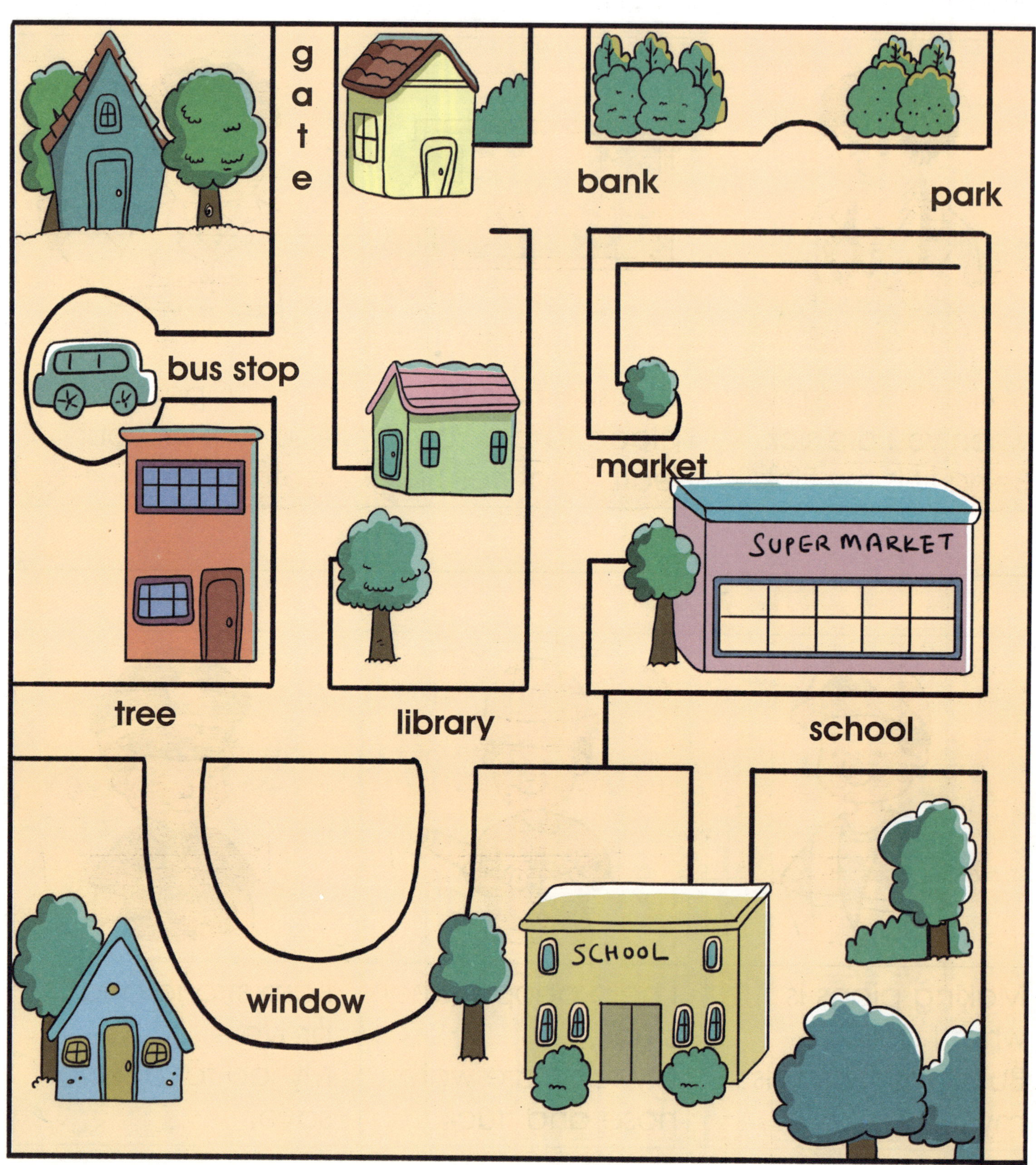

Words that Name Animals

Unscramble the words to find the names of animals that popped out of the magician's hat.

Were you a magician, what would you say to pop animals out of your bag? To solve the riddle, arrange the letters below in the given order.

R	A	A	B	B	R	A	D	A
1	2	3	4	5	6	7	8	9

_	_	_	_	_	_	_	_	_
2	4	1	3	8	7	5	6	9

Words that Name Things

Use the code to decode the words that name things.

A – @	B – #	C – $	D – %	E – ^	F – &	G – *	H – (	I –)
J – =	K – +	L – >	M – <	N – ?	O – "	P – }	Q – {	R – [
S –]	T – o	U – \	V – /	W – £	X – ©	Y – ÷	Z – ±	

1. > @ < }

____ ____ ____ ____

2. # [\ ] (

____ ____ ____ ____ ____

3. $ @ < ^ [@

____ ____ ____ ____ ____ ____

4.] " @ }

____ ____ ____ ____

5. } @) >

____ ____ ____ ____

6. $ > " $ +

____ ____ ____ ____ ____

7. [" } ^

____ ____ ____ ____

8. O)]] \ ^

____ ____ ____ ____ ____ ____

Word Association

Draw lines to match the words that name things to the place they belong.

Use a word from above to complete each sentence.

1. Look at the little boy playing on the ____________.
2. Grandma gave me a story ____________.
3. Glue the ____________ on the postcard.
4. I can hear the ____________ ringing.
5. Miss Lee drew a line with a ____________.
6. Lisa broke a ____________ ____________.
7. The lamp is beside the ____________.
8. The ____________ flew high in the sky.

BONUS BOX

Write names of two things with letter S you find in the kitchen.

Words that Name Fruits

Read the clues and complete the crossword puzzle.

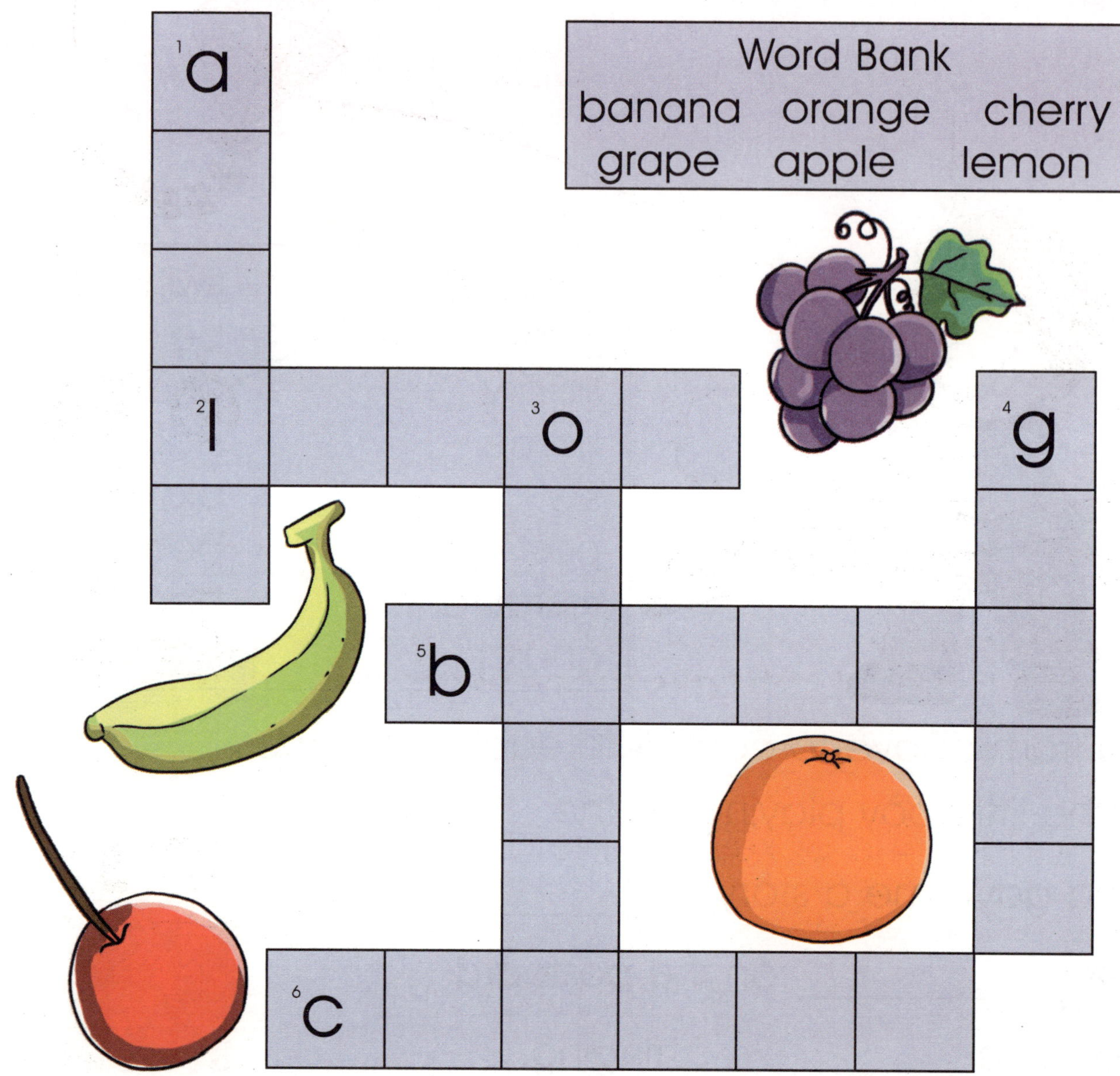

Across

2. I am a round, yellow fruit.
5. I am a long, yellow fruit.
6. I am red. I often hang from trees in pairs.

Down

1. I can be red, yellow or green.
3. I am the colour of a basketball.
4. I hang in bunches from vines.

BONUS BOX

I am sour and look like an orange. The word tangy comes from my name. What am I?

Transport Words

The words in bold are incorrect. Correct the words with the help of each picture and write the most suitable answer above each word.

car

1. Mother drives her **boat** to the office.

2. Daddy gifted a **bus** on Mac's birthday.

3. The princess went to the ball in a **airplane**.

4. People used to travel in **trucks** many years ago.

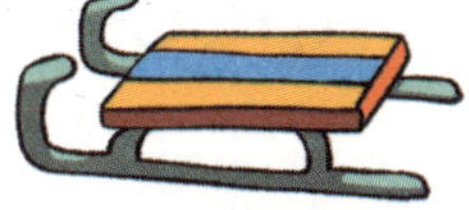

5. The men loaded the boxes into the **bicycle**.

6. We are waiting for the school **train**.

7. The **ship** will soon take off from the airport.

8. A **tram** carries a lot of people to far off places.

BONUS BOX

What is it that has three colours and controls vehicles on road?

Word Association

Cross out the word or words in each group that is not related to the words in bold.

1. Toys
top
doll
eraser
slides

2. Pets
fish
lion
rabbit
cat

3. Market
shops
grocer
ink
booth

4. Food
popcorn
jam
kettle
marble

5. School
bell
desk
classroom
mittens

6. Insects
bee
ant
butterfly
snail

7. Sports
tennis
soccer
football
stumps

8. Footwear
shoes
socks
floaters
bellies

9. Cutlery
spoon
fork
knife
mat

BONUS BOX

Choose any 4 letters from S, H, E, F, C, O and write a word that names a drink.

It's a Good Night!

Look at each picture and write what each person is saying. Use the words from the word bank below.

Hello	Good night	Sorry	Thank you	Excuse me

1. ______________, may I speak to John?

2. ______________ Mummy.

3. May I have some water, ______________?

4. ______________ Daddy.

5. ______________ Miss Mary.

Action Words

Words that show an action or work are called action words.
Run, **fly** and **talk** are action words.

Read each word in the spaces below. If it is an action word, colour it green. If it is not an action word, colour it yellow.

pencil
book
two
kick
six
add
swim
a
run
make
skip
flour
works
sleep
I
bed
jump
green
talk
sit
old
she
tree
bird

Action Words

Complete the sentences using a word from the word box.

1. Jane and Kim ______________ a game.

2. Jane ______________ the board.

3. She ______________ a picture.

4. Jane ______________ Kim a riddle.

5. Kim ______________ a book.

6. He likes to ______________ riddle books.

7. Jane ______________ to twenty.

8. Just then, Kim ______________ the riddle.

Play Time!

Sort these words and write them under the matching group.

jump	mew	look	run	speak	write	watch	chew
walk	neigh	chirp	draw	yell	weep	clap	

Animals in Action

What can these animals do? Tick the correct answers in the boxes given.

1. A horse can ____________ skip gallop
2. A cow can ____________ moo coo

3. A parrot can ____________ talk growl
4. A rabbit can ____________ hop jump
5. A hamster can ____________ whistle squeak
6. A hen can ____________ cluck crow
7. A snail can ____________ slide crawl
8. A duck can ____________ giggle quack

Opposites

Read each word and match the opposites.

A Cold Treat?

Use the word bank and write opposites for words below.

Word Bank:

on far false win hard quiet close dirty deep thin

1. clean ____________
2. near ____________
3. off ____________
4. noisy ____________
5. shallow ____________
6. true ____________
7. thin ____________
8. lose ____________
9. soft ____________
10. open ____________

BONUS BOX

Write an opposite for the word **stale**. Then write a sentence with the word

On the Grill

How do these food items taste? Choose food items and their taste and write them in the boxes below.

orange
salty
honey
sweet
lemon
sour
coffee
chillies
spicy
pretzels
tangy
bitter

BONUS BOX

Which is your favourite fruit? How does it taste?

How Does it Feel?

Match each picture to the correct word that describes how it might feel.

How Do You Feel?

Choose a word from the word box and write it for the matching face.

angry	happy	sad	worried	scared
surprised	confused	overjoyed	upset	

____________ ____________ ____________

____________ ____________ ____________

____________ ____________ ____________

Words to Describe

Tick (√) the word in each group that describes each picture.

1. tiny hairy fat
2. pretty petals stem
3. silly funny loving
4. pet fast wild
5. short round new
6. old dirty shirt

Rhyming Words

Words that sound the same at the end are called rhyming words.
For example: pair-hair, jelly-belly, ate-late

Circle the words in each group that rhyme.

1. horn comb corn hen
2. tree bee peas seen
3. spoon cool stoop moon
4. fly bow tie say
5. clock yolk sock tall
6. wool wear full bun
7. cloak brown song down
8. ink pluck pick stick

Analogies

An analogy is a comparison of two pairs of words that are related in a similar way.
For example: **bird** is to **sky** as **fish** is to **water**

Complete each analogy using a word from the word box.

1. Bus is to road as boat is to ____________ .

2. Stars are to night as sun is to ____________ .

3. Straw is to drink as spoon is to ____________ .

4. Cap is to head as shoes is to ____________ .

5. Blue is to sky as red is to ____________ .

6. King is to man as queen is to ____________ .

7. Toe is to foot as finger is to ____________ .

8. Grapes is to fruit as peas is to ____________ .

BONUS BOX

Make your own pairs of analogies and quiz your friends.
Write any two pairs here.

Words Often Confused

Tick the correct answers in the boxes below.

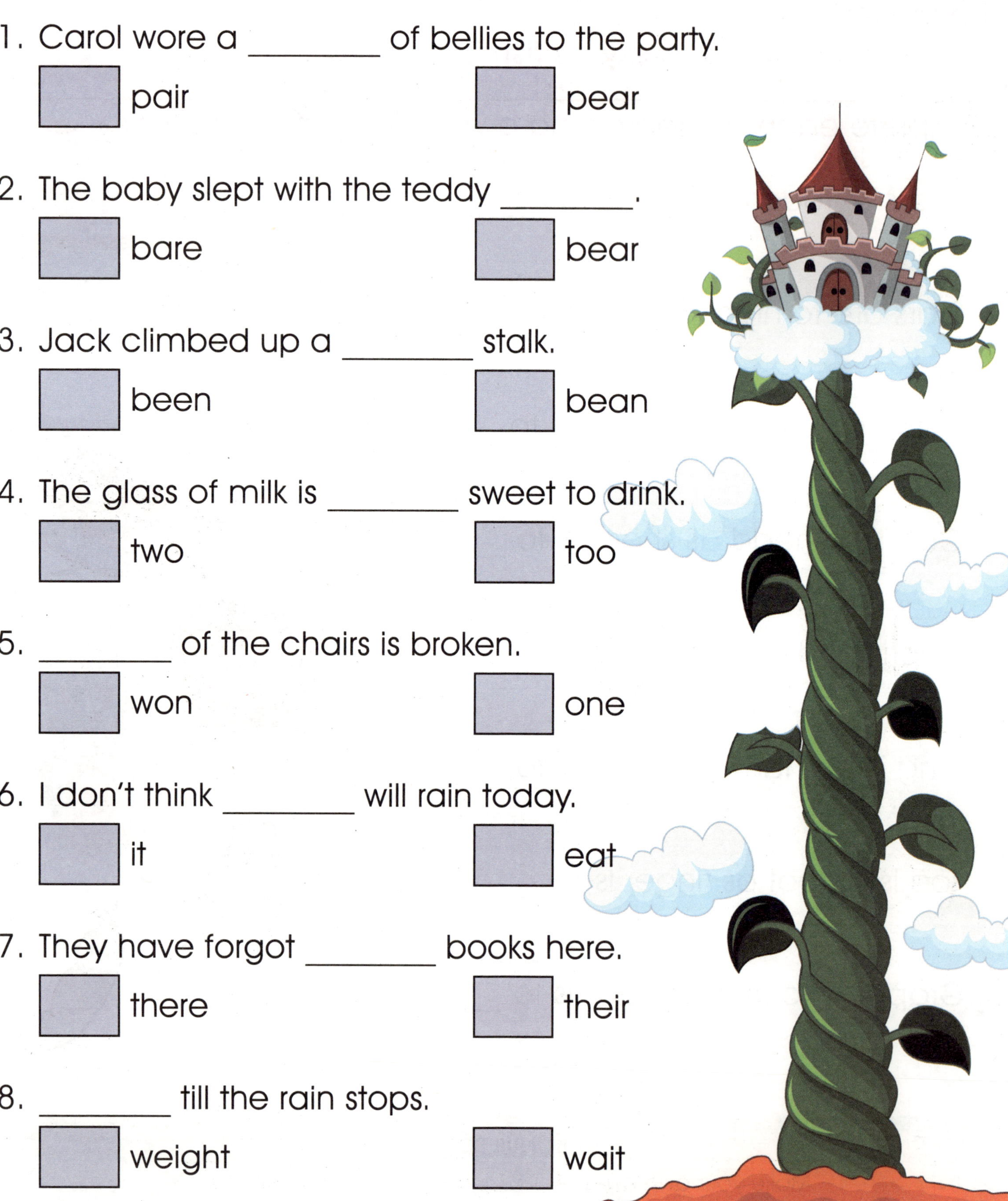

1. Carol wore a ________ of bellies to the party.

   ☐ pair ☐ pear

2. The baby slept with the teddy ________.

   ☐ bare ☐ bear

3. Jack climbed up a ________ stalk.

   ☐ been ☐ bean

4. The glass of milk is ________ sweet to drink.

   ☐ two ☐ too

5. ________ of the chairs is broken.

   ☐ won ☐ one

6. I don't think ________ will rain today.

   ☐ it ☐ eat

7. They have forgot ________ books here.

   ☐ there ☐ their

8. ________ till the rain stops.

   ☐ weight ☐ wait

Who's the Winner?

Play this game with your friends and help the children reach the school.

Start

What do you write with?

Where do you wear a backpack?

What do we use to cut cloth?

What do you use to stick things?

What takes you to school?

What days do you go to school?

Who do you see when you are sick?

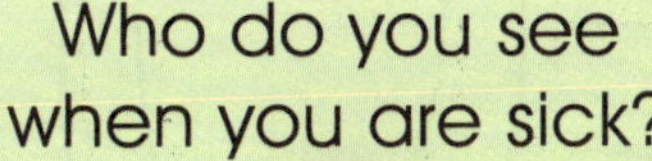

Which game is this?

What tells us the time?

What do you sit on?

Where do you find books and read quietly?

Finish

Answer Key

Page 2

Across
1 head
4. mouth
6. ears
7. eyes
8. nose

Down
1. hair
2. bones
3. legs
5. hands.

Page 3

1. hair
2. waist
3. finger
4. neck
5. wrist
6. shoulder
7. palm
8. feet

Page 4

1. trunk
2. tentacles
3. fins
4. beak
5. shell

Page 5

Words that name people are:
father, boy, girl, mother

Page 6

a	b	c	d	e	f	g	j	h	s
i	s	o	c	k	s	j	a	k	h
l	k	m	o	n	o	p	c	q	i
r	i	p	a	n	t	s	k	s	r
t	r	u	t	v	w	x	e	y	t
z	t	a	b	c	d	e	t	f	g
h	i	j	k	l	m	n	o	p	q
t	i	e	r	s	t	h	a	t	u

Page 7

doctor
teacher
dentist
architect
fire fighter
policeman

Page 8

Page 9

1. rabbit
2. snake
3. ostrich
4. crab
5. monkey
6. frog
7. sheep
8. mouse
9. turtle
10. penguin

Page 10

1. lamp
2. brush
3. camera
4. soap
5. pail
6. clock
7. rope
8. tissue

Answer Key

Page 11

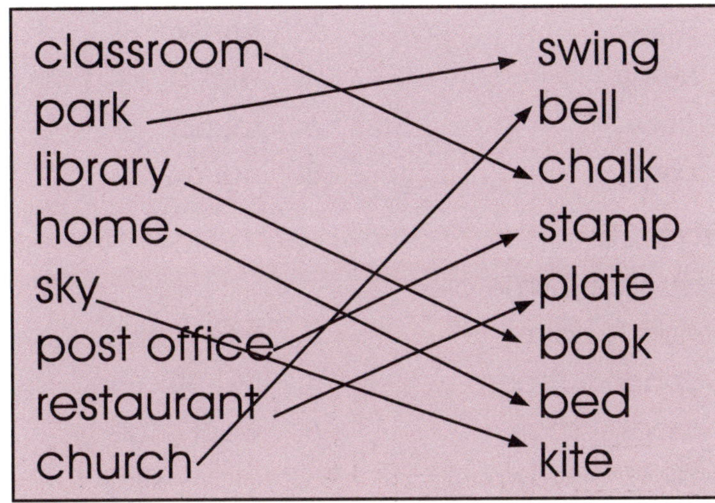

1.	swing	2.	book
3.	stamp	4.	bell
5.	chalk	6.	plate
7.	bed	8.	kite

Page 12

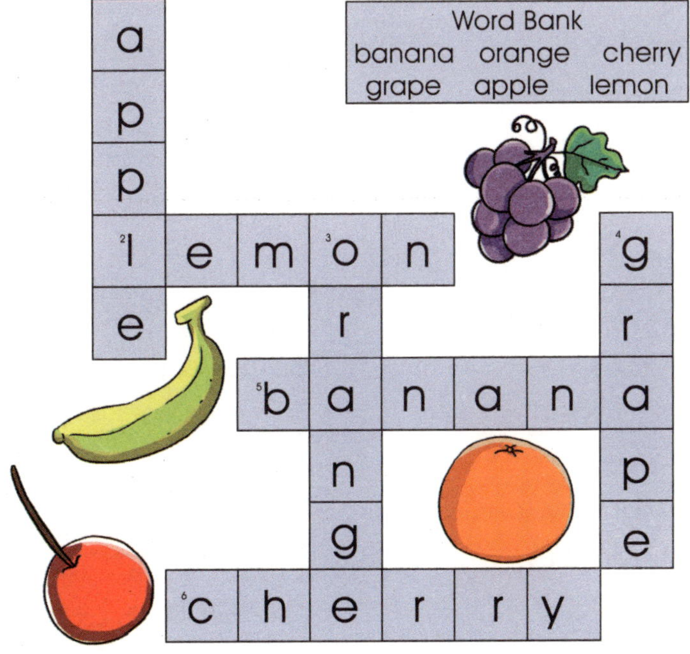

Page 13

1.	car	2.	bicycle
3.	wagon	4.	sleigh
5.	truck	6.	bus
7.	airplane	8.	train

Page 14

1.	eraser, slides	2.	lion
3.	ink	4.	kettle
5.	mittens	6.	snail
7.	stumps	8.	socks
9.	mat		

Page 15

1.	Hello	2.	Sorry
3.	Please	4.	Good night
5.	Excuse me		

Page 16

Action words are: kick, swim, run, sleep, work, talk, sit, jump, skip, make, add

Page 17

1.	play	2.	cleans
3.	draws	4.	asks
5.	gets	6.	read
7.	counts	8.	solves

Page 18

1.	weep, look, watch	2.	draw, clap, write
3.	mew, neigh, chirp	4.	jump, walk, run
5.	speak, chew, yell		

Page 19

1.	gallop	2.	moo
3.	talk	4.	hop
5.	squeak	6.	cluck
7.	crawl	8.	quack

Page 20

1.	hot – cold	2.	short – tall
3.	sad – happy	4.	day – night
5.	old – new	6.	big – little

Page 21

1.	clean – dirty	2.	near – far
3.	off – on	4.	noisy – quiet
5.	shallow – deep	6.	true – false
7.	thin – thick	8.	lose – win
9.	soft – hard	10.	open – close

Answer Key

Page 22

1. orange – tangy
2. honey – sweet
3. lemon – sour
4. coffee – bitter
5. chillies – spicy
6. pretzels – salty

Page 23

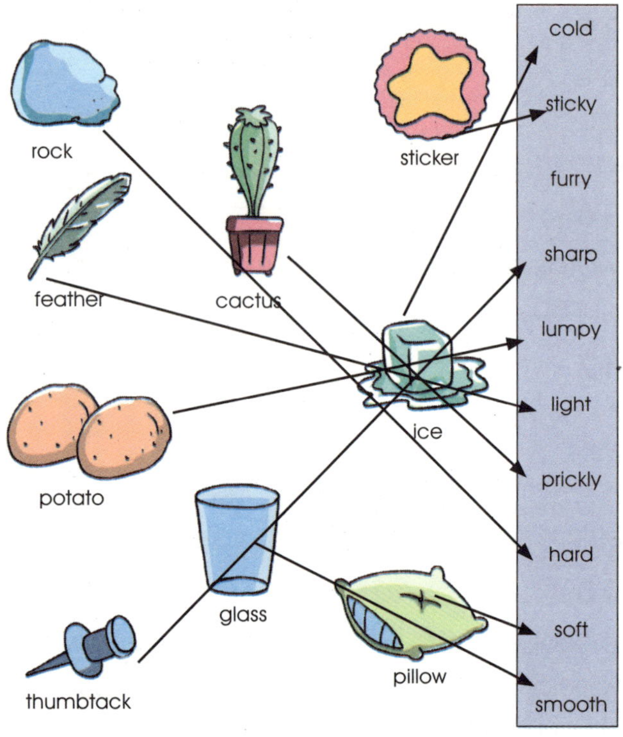

Page 24

Page 25

1. hairy
2. pretty
3. funny
4. wild
5. curly
6. round
7. dirty
8. narrow

Page 26

Words that rhyme are:

1. horn – corn
2. tree – bee
3. spoon – moon
4. fly – tie
5. clock – sock
6. wool – full
7. brown – down
8. pick – stick

Page 27

1. water
2. day
3. food
4. feet
5. apple
6. woman
7. hand
8. vegetables

Page 28

1. pair
2. bear
3. bean
4. too
5. one
6. it
7. their
8. wait

Page 29

The answers are:

1. pencil/pen
2. teacher
3. shoulder
4. scissors
5. glue
6. bus
7. Monday to Friday
8. Doctor
9. Football
10. Clock
11. Chair
12. library